Thoughts & Musings
Life, Love, and The Human Condition

P.K. Rankin

FAIRVIEW PRESS MEDIA

This limited edition of

Thoughts & Musings

Life, Love, and The Human Condition

By P.K. Rankin

Has been privately printed,

and individually signed

by the author

Copyright © 2023 P.K. Rankin

All rights reserved.

No part of this book may be reproduced, or stored in a retrieval system, or transmitted in any form or by any means, electronic, mechanical, photocopying, recording, or otherwise, without the express written permission of the publisher.

Cover design by: VLSK *for* Fairview Press Media Mgt.

Illustrations by: Cesar Lista & Judy Rogers
& Vickie L Sargent-Kler

ISBN:9798870132945
Printed in the United States of America

DEDICATION

These poems are dedicated to my family and
my best friends for never allowing me to give
up on my passion for writing and expressing my gifts.

To the world at large for never making it easy,
but always making it an adventure.

To my Lord and Savior Jesus Christ for blessing
me beyond measure with love, family, friends, life, and the
challenges therein.

The journey continues.

CONTENTS

Preface

LIFE

1	Life	Pg 3
2	The Author	Pg 5
3	Feelings	Pg 7
4	Freedom is Messy	Pg 8
5	No Heroes	Pg 11
6	Merchant Marine	Pg 13
7	The Final Passage	Pg 15
8	Start Living	Pg 17
9	Ma Maw	Pg 20
10	To Dad on His Birthday	Pg 22

LOVE

11	Are You There	Pg 27
12	Lament For Love	Pg 29
13	Deep	Pg 33
14	The Point	Pg 35
15	My Love	Pg 37
16	The Search for Love	Pg 41
17	The Victory of True Love	Pg 43
18	A Passing Love	Pg 45

19	The Light of Love	Pg 47
20	Love and Parting	Pg 49
21	My Love for Thee	Pg 51
22	Unlock the Door	Pg 53

THE HUMAN CONDITION

23	The Standard	Pg 57
24	The Heart of Man	Pg 59
25	Woman	Pg 61
26	Those Times	Pg 63
27	Pity	Pg 65
28	The Battle	Pg 67
29	The Game	Pg 71
30	My Son	Pg 73
31	The Heart	Pg 75
32	The Last Knight	Pg 79
33	Feelings of Thought	Pg 81
34	The Final Hour	Pg 83

About the Author

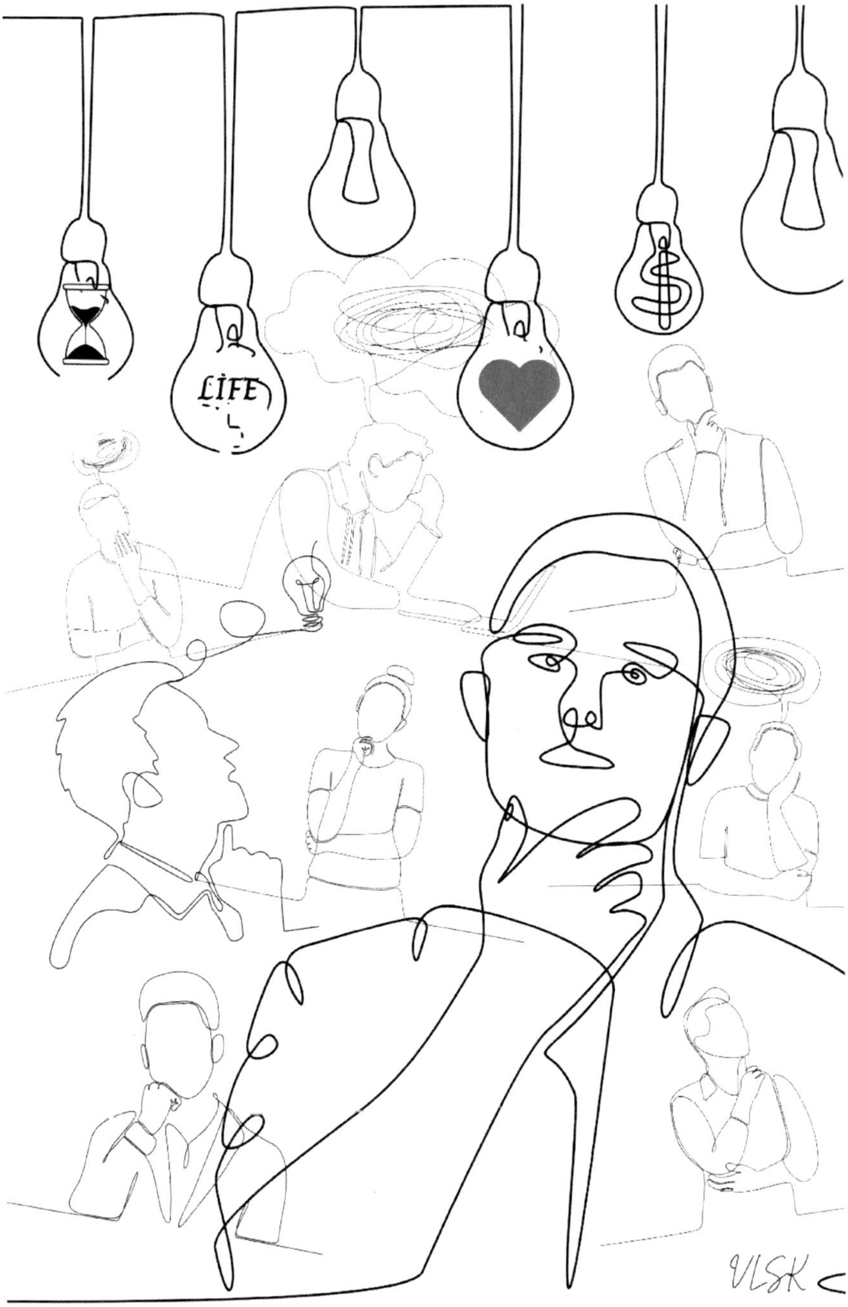
LIFE

PREFACE

What you will find in the following pages are the collected thoughts and musings of my life that I managed to capture in writing. I have more writings that are yet unfinished that lie about my office or in folders that have yet to become full-fledged tales of the short or long variety. I took a brief time over the past year to rifle through these bits of myself and realized that they needed to breathe and shared with others. Here, they are ready for your personal enjoyment or your private condemnation, as the mood may strike you. Keep in mind, however, that they are just thoughts and musings, not doctrine. I hope, regardless of your temperament, that you will read and reread them as you ponder your own thoughts on the subjects. Take them in and meld them with your own and other's thoughts as you contemplate life, love, and the human condition from your own perch. We are, after all, only human and any thought that inspires us to our own, quickens our heart, or challenges our intransigence is something to be savored. Thank you for joining me on this journey.

LIFE

In working to categorize these poems for this publication. I found that without really thinking about it; I had learned so much over the course of the past thirty-plus years. I look at our world today and see so little compassion or understanding for others, and I realize that life teaches us so much when we open our hearts, minds, and eyes. These poems are some of my thoughts on life over the years. From the 1980s to the present, each one is a tiny time capsule reflecting my level of understanding at that moment in time. Times of crisis or transition as well as observational commentaries inspired by world events or family milestones, are here for review. Take them for what they are. I hope these inspire your own introspection or consideration in moments great and small.

P.K. Rankin

Life by Cesar Lista

LIFE

What is life? The layman asked,
and how am I to find it?
Amidst the ruins of time, I stand
unwilling to submit.

For knowledge does the scholar plead;
a fortress for to build.
Impervious by his decree
to any mind unskilled.

Forever and anon we search,
for meaning to our life.
With government and vaulted church
we seek to quell the strife.

Yet like a fire to end a fire,
the vision is consumed.
The secret side of man's desire
escorts him to his doom.

P.K. Rankin

The Author by Cesar Lista

THE AUTHOR

Each day only a page in the book of our lives. Merely a spot of ink on the grand pages of history. And yet, at the same time, each second, we live is an entire microcosm unto itself. Whence we come has no bearing, our destination left to God. Still, each breath may be our last, each man may be a friend, and who can say how you might change another through your own life.

Let us then leave history to its Dark Grave and tomorrow to unfold as it will. Think you of the moment at hand and allow it to be a herald for the moment to come, another word in that book, a testimony to your direction and remember always that when the last second comes and our Lord closes your book, your authorship will speak for itself.

Are you writing a short story or a novel, fact, or fiction?
Check each word.
Your answer lies there.

Feelings by Cesar Lista

FEELINGS

There is a time in every life when decisions must be made. A time to lay aside the childish dreams of youth and clothe oneself in the garments of adulthood. There is no escaping this inevitable "Day of Reckoning" for it comes unbidden to every one of us, stealing into our fantasy world of happiness with the stealth of a tiger. No, you can't run from this moment, for once it is upon you, it holds you tight, unwilling to relinquish its grip even unto death. What, then, shall I do you ask? Shall I lose my dreams and give myself over to this new responsibility? No, I say, you must learn to master this new you. You must make this your ally and use it to your benefit. "When I was no longer a child, I put away childish things". Hold on to your dreams and never give away that small part of you which remains a child forever. At the same time, however, put away the mannerisms of childhood and take up the miter of responsibility, accept with great joy the obligations and the rewards of adult life.

It is our dreams which give each of us a certain spark of individuality; it is our dreams which give us a goal for this life. Hold on to your dreams and trust in God. Make your plans and lead your life as you should. Through it all, however, remember that LIFE has a purpose for each of us, no matter how small, and it is this purpose which we must find, in our dreams or in the Cold, Hard Reality of LIFE. Don't let it sneak up and smack you in the face some day. You be the one to seek out your purpose, grip it by the throat and be the master of your destiny. In short, don't let life master you. You be one of the few who rise above the crowd and master life.

Freedom is Messy by VickieLSK

FREEDOM IS MESSY

Freedom is Messy! It's Hard and demanding!
To keep it you've got to be willing to stand!
Opposing the tyrant, bent on control,
or the apparatchik who poisons your soul.

Freedom is Messy! It's worth more than gold!
It should never be bartered, surrendered, or sold!
Each generation must win it anew;
with vigilance, courage, and sacrifice too!

Thoughts & Musings

Freedom is Messy! It never comes free!
It's not for the fearful who live on their knees;
scared of the pain they'll have to endure,
certain that chains are the preferable cure.

Freedom is Messy! It's built on respect!
For neighbors and others you haven't met yet.
We accept other's creeds and religious convictions.
We suffer their words and their horrid opinions.

Freedom is Messy! God made it that way!
He gave us a conscience and free will to say;
"This is the line! Your control ends here!
Life and liberty, we hold to be dear!"

Freedom is Messy! In providence founded!
Our republic, in God's word, was heavily grounded!
Outside of His grace, it's just like all the others.
The rights of mankind it now seeks to smother!
Freedom is worth every drop of blood used
to water the tree of liberty's roots.
Our ancestor's volunteered fathers and sons
who struggled and died so they were not the ones;

to watch as the light of liberty died
believing the tyrant's unbearable lies;
that we are not free, we belong to the system.
They'll provide us a way for life and subsistence.

It's our turn now to stand forth and say,
"we won't permit freedom to perish this way"!
Steadfast and true on the battle's front line,
It's our blood defending freedom this time.

Yes!
Freedom is Messy! It is bought with a price!
We learned from Jesus, our savior, The Christ!

No Heroes by Cesar Lista

NO HEROES

To speak words, you are not free to speak,
To think thoughts, you are not free to have.
To take actions you are forbidden to take.
To question those who purport to rule over you.
To forswear that authority and forge ahead on the path of free will.

To desire what has been taken and pursue what you are denied.
To detest what is evil when it is peddled as righteous.
To disclaim what is hurtful when we are told that it heals.
To refuse the exchange of freedom for promised security.
To welcome the reaper and refuse the raiment of the slave.

There is no favor given to the one who takes the untrodden path.
There is no gratitude for the intrepid soul who remains steadfast in the face of tyranny.
There is no parade for victory today; only the next assault to be met by the vigilant.
There are no heroes in the eternal struggle for the freedom of mankind.
All that remains are those who struggle for freedom and those who have accepted their chains.

P.K. Rankin

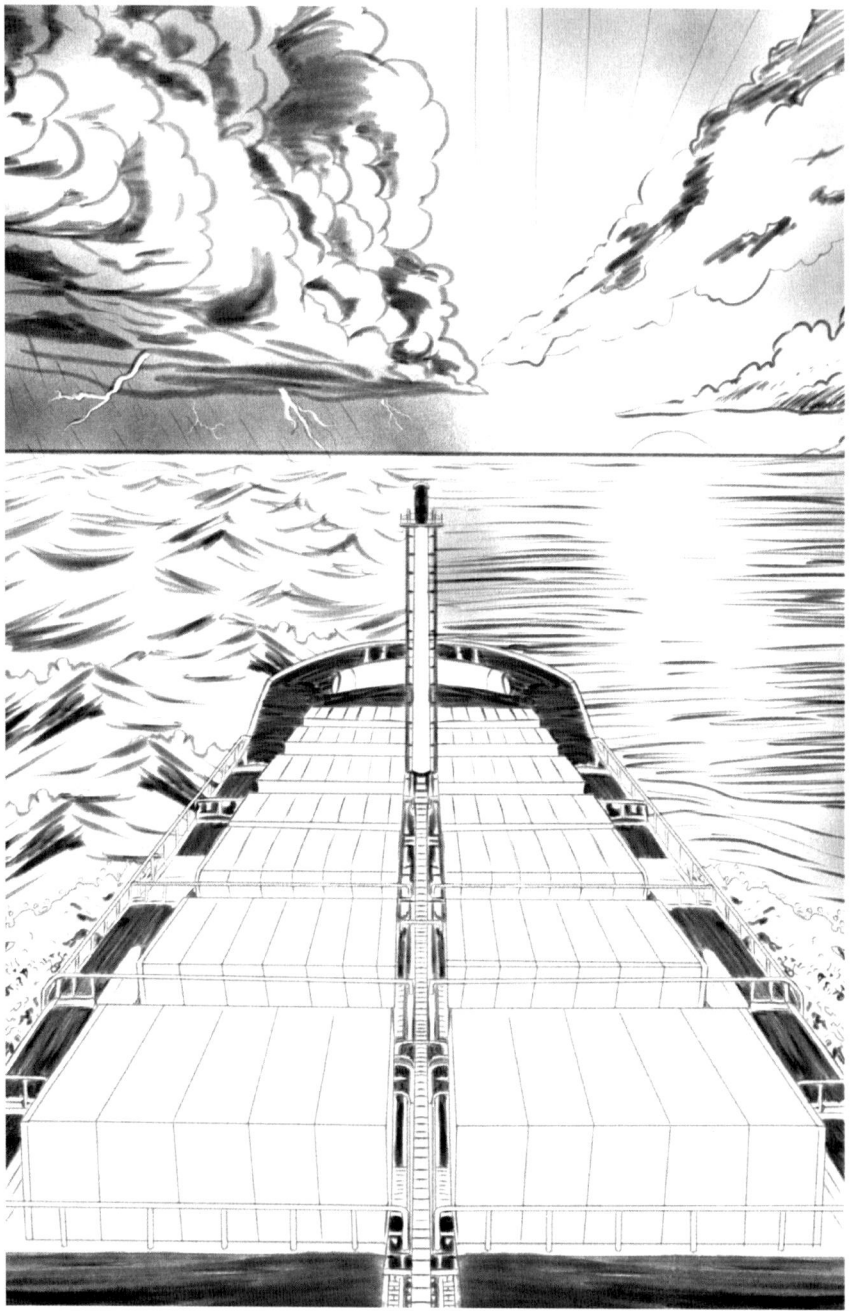

Merchant Marine by Cesar Lista

MERCHANT MARINE

As morning brings the flooding tide
we set sail for ports of call.
With God and wind upon our side
the goods of the world we haul.

For centuries we have endured
the endless perils of the sea.
Our place in history assured
for all the charted world to see.

To be mariners we have aspired
we chose a noble life.
Though many women we admire
the ocean is our wife.

We journey forth to ply our trade
in a world of restless times.
Like those before us we stand proud
'til the storm at last subsides.

The Final Passage by Cesar Lista

THE FINAL PASSAGE

They set the sails to meet the tide
As once again the waves she'll ride.
With time ashore the men heave to
And say goodbye to lovers true.

From day to day and port to port
Their lady makes the passage short.
Until the day the last load goes
And men of the sea head home once more.

Through hills of green the lady plies
Guided on by the somber eyes
Of men whose life belongs to thee;
Their choice in life has been the sea.

The passage long the sea is rough.
The men are strong the ship is tough.
At times their life is breath-to-breath.
Time and again the sea brings death.

But when at last the lines are cast
And the gangway hits the shore
There will come a day when time has passed
And the Captain sails no more.

A nature strange for a Lady Fair
To harden the skin and gray the hair.
Still, on we'll sail 'til our day arrives
And the final passage ends our lives.

Men of the sea we are today!
Men of the sea 'til our dying day!

START LIVING

We spend a fair portion of our lives wading on the edges of our existence. Always too tentative about the unknown emotions, and the known fears, that we harbor in our souls; to actually experience complete success or failure. We pad our falls with the falsehoods we tell ourselves, and we shore up our daily lives with the shared platitudes of friends, coworkers, and family. But ultimately, it's all about our own fears. We are fully capable of diving into life to challenge the prospect of sinking or swimming, but it's much safer in the shallow end. So, we stay there where even a catastrophe won't drown us. We accept the safe job, the uncontroversial or known relationships and the careful existence; that's always the most comfortable. Let's be honest, when it comes right down to it, we all want to be comfortable, don't we? It's not about being happy for us, but truly, we are creatures of comfort and habit.

We will wallow in the mire and the self-pity of our lives until the commonness of the situation saps our energy; destroys our ability to form a cogent thought and removes the last drop of free will from our spirit. But we steadfastly refuse to take a risk or make a change that might make those around us uncomfortable or skeptical of our decision-making skills. We tell ourselves endlessly that it's all about being responsible or convincing ourselves that we just don't have the heart to hurt those around us; but actually, we don't want to feel uncomfortable ourselves. We don't want others questioning our decisions or speculating on our motives, so we dodge the change again.

We pat ourselves on the back for being thoughtful and considerate of others; while the whole time we forge ahead ignoring our own needs, be they emotional, intellectual, spiritual or physical. The truth is that we've all learned to permit others to be inconsiderate of us, but we wouldn't dare reciprocate. There's no need to be purposefully inconsiderate of others. But there's also no requirement to allow the world to expect everything from you and deny you anything in return.

When's the last time your friend actually asked where you were, and how you were doing? While actually expecting you to provide an honest, unvarnished response about yourself as a person at that moment in time? More importantly, when is the last time you gave that honest answer and your friend or family member actually listened to the answer without criticizing you for not providing the answer and reasoning they expected you to have?

Stop living at the shallow end of life.

Stop dreaming big and living small for the sake of comfort and approval.

Stop giving all of the answers that everyone expects you to give and start giving the answers you truly believe in your heart and soul.

In short, my friend, start living!

Thoughts & Musings

Start Living by Cesar Lista

P.K. Rankin

MA MAW

Ma Maw
(Grandma Kentucky Style)

I sometimes wonder who you were?
A lovely young country girl, carefree
and unfettered by the cold chains of
city life. Perhaps a solemn young lady
bound by the ties of family and the duties
of a wife.

On occasion I hear the clear note of youth
in that voice made weary by time. There are
pictures on the wall to remind us that you
haven't always been a grandma and a wealth of
stories full of wisdom to teach us those lessons
learned through time.

Still, in the midst of my wanderings I see that
loving face I know so well. The sparkle is still
in those eyes and the voice, though weary with
time, still speaks volumes about the love in that
Grand Heart.

I see the wrinkles, evidence of the trials and
tribulations that life has offered, and I am
humbled to think of how little I can know
compared to the wisdom which must reside in that
precious soul.

The gray hair, worn as proudly as any soldier
might wear his medal of honor, says you've earned
your place of respect in this family; your place of
honor in our hearts. The look of concern on your

brow evident with each word of advice, tells me I
am always on your mind, a loved one not forgotten
in the hustle of this world.

I may wander far and wide from my "Old Kentucky
Home", maybe contemplate the past.
But you're always with me Ma Ma, at the first
and at the last.

P.K. Rankin

TO DAD ON HIS BIRTHDAY

Today is a day of Heroes when we remember the Harbor at Pearl.
Today, each good American will display his flag unfurled.
We mourn the lost and praise those who remain and each
of us recites a prayer 'twill never happen again.

That's the day outside this house, in the place beyond our walls.
Another time does come to mind whene'er this day does fall.
We look back through the years to a day not far displaced.
We celebrate the day when Grandma gazed upon your face.

To those who do not know you, it's another day at best,
another fleeting moment in a world which knows no rest.
To most, it's just another day, a good day at its' best.

Time marched on and burdens came. You bore them one and all.
When fatherhood came much too soon, you answered to the call.
No matter the sacrifice required, you made it without complaint.
No task could steer you from your course. You never said I can't.

Steadfast in the face of life you've given without reserve.
And much to my dismay, dear Dad, you don't have half
 what you deserve.
Still, you never asked for mansions or the yachts and autos fine.
You've always given all you had to make this family shine.

I want you to know I Love you for your selfless care and guidance.
No, Son could ask a greater man to build his confidence.
No card could say these words to you. No gift I could find
would suffice.
Dear father, if it were in my power, I would gladly grow up twice.

So HAPPY BIRTHDAY FATHER you have earned this day so well.
The worth of the gifts you've given me no man could ever tell.

Thoughts & Musings

I salute you with my heart and with pride only a son can feel.
I thank the Lord for the friend I have; no man may ever steal.

I LOVE YOU FATHER

LOVE

We've all been there. Love, in all its veiled and unveiled forms, has touched us in some way over the course of our lives. There is a siren, or a muse connected to every single poem in this section. I must say that despite the ups and downs of love, I find myself looking back and understanding the joy and the pain of being a part of our growth as human beings. The joy of love shared dulls the pain of previously unrequited or lost love in the same way as those losses intensify the joy of love shared. Love isn't a vending machine. I believed as a young man that love was somehow an entitlement for each of us. While I believe we are each worthy of love, I have come to understand that love is like respect; something earned and crafted as opposed to something we merely pick up at the checkout. The only love in the universe that you get without earning or meriting it is the love of God. Even the love of a parent is not a guarantee for many, but every single person who lives, has lived, or will live on this planet, born or unborn, is loved by God. That puts the rest of it in context.

P.K. Rankin

Are You There by VickieLSK

ARE YOU THERE

I call to you with the song of my heart.
And yet no answer.
Can you not feel the Love inside me?
Seeking you, crying out to you from within?

Are you there?

Endlessly, I search with my eyes,
But to no avail.
Am I to rely merely on chance?
Perhaps a twisted whim of fate?
No!
It is not with my eyes that I will find you.

I ask again.
Are you there?

I have seen you before, in a dream.
Not your physical beauty, but the truth
of you. And still I wonder, Are you there?
Or merely a creation of my own desire?
I await your answer.

LAMENT FOR LOVE

My heart is heavily laden, burdened with a longing for the
things that I cannot have.
The silken feel of a lover's touch, the sweet melody of her
voice calling my name.
Cannot? You ask, and why is that?

I know this to be true, for my eyes are blinded to the
language of her movement.
My heart is hardened to the beckoning of her soul.
My mind is dumb to the words of her mouth and all, at last
 depends on these.

It is a terrible affliction, I fear; one for which there is no cure.
For although the depths of my love cannot be measured,
nor the bounds of my love be charted,
neither can I put forth these endless feelings in tangible manner.
Alas, I fear 'twill never be.

The one I seek might cross my path a hundred times a thousand.
Yet, I, the fool, in all respects might never know the truth.
Might it be that I, languid in my living as I am in all respects,
shall evermore be consigned to an existence of singular vacuity.

Nay, I think not.
For even in the midst of my despair, Love has found me out.
Lighting on my shoulder and whispering into my ear.
that hope is not lost.

P.K. Rankin

It is only now,
in the presence of LOVE itself,
that I can truly see the constancy of Love.

It is only now,
warmed by its flame,
that my heart is released from its bonds of stone.

It is only now,
Engulfed in its power,
that my mind is freed from it's prison
of ignoble character
and set upon the wind to soar.

Sadly,
it is only now,
surrounded by its peace,
that I can say with kindness and compassion
that search as you may,
LOVE is not a treasure to be unearthed.

In the final analysis,
it is an emotion of wisdom and purpose;
seeking each of us in its own time.

Love, my friend,
will find you too if you will, but be still
and await it's coming.

LOVE will find you out.

Thoughts & Musings

Lament for Love by Cesar Lista

P.K. Rankin

Deep by VickieLSK

DEEP

From day to day, I contemplate,
The separate roads we tread.
We take a chance or risk the wait,
And hope for Love ahead.

A Love of Joy, A Love that burns.
In life, the key to all.
To left and right we often turn,
Sometimes we take the fall.

Yet in the end to fall we seek,
To fall so deep in Love.
'Tis someone kind and true we seek,
Alas, the one true Love.

The Point by Cesar Lista

THE POINT

They say sometimes this youth of mine
Is wasted on the young.
But, I believe, as they perceive,
That life is far too short.

We live our days an endless haze.
Of plateaus to the top.
If madness is as madness does,
We've simply missed the point.

We didn't pass it by, alas
It's been there all along.
We seem to find more fun in lies,
My God, I think we're lost!

When Love is gone, our life drags on,
The truth we merely drop.
What need of truth, why value youth,
We've simply missed the point.

The point, you ask, what sort of task
Is this, you have in mind?
I didn't miss it. The point is this:
The Heart of Life is Love!

MY LOVE

As from afar, I see thy face,
a sweet and radiant child.
My life may be at last complete
if thou wouldst stay a while.

Linger, but a moment more and
grace me with thy smile.

In day thou art the fairest flower
of any in the field.
At night the glow of yonder moon
is ever thine to wield.

The stars shall be a cloak
for thee, the sun shall be
thy shield.

From whence thee came I may not know,
thy path is thine to see.
And where thou goest thou will
not show whene'r thou leavest me.

Still, I ask if thou wilt stay
and never let me be.

Would that our two hearts may be
in love, forever bound.
'Tis well I know, a truer love shall
nevermore be found.

'Tis well I know, a truer love
shall never come around.

What then shall I say to thee
that thou might know my love?
What more can a man reveal to
God and Heaven above?

Might a man conceal himself
from this wondrous thing called
love?

Of thee I will ask nothing more
than only this to hear.
In this world's life, compared
to thee, nothing is more dear.

So, take my hand and stay my
love that I may never fear.

Thoughts & Musings

My Love by Cesar List

P.K. Rankin

The Search for Love by Judy Rogers

THE SEARCH FOR LOVE

Where, my dear, shall I look for Love;
In meadows fair and mountains high?
Or shall I leave this wandering life
And seek Love in your peaceful sigh?

Does Love reside on rambling trails;
Along the highways traveled much?
Might it be that Love resides
In the tenderness of your sweet touch?

Must I traverse the oceans deep;
Spend my life upon the seas?
Or could it be your smile, my dear,
Is greater still than all of these?

Across the skies my Love I seek;
To Heaven's very door.
Could it be true the Love I seek
Is in this world no more?

Surely not. I know it false,
The telling only lies.
For I have found the Love I seek;
'Tis shining in your eyes.

The Victory of True Love by VickieLSK

Thoughts & Musings

THE VICTORY OF TRUE LOVE

We raise a glass to victory and gaze into the sun.
The world's been hard on you and me and still, at last, we've won.

We didn't take the easy road or slip around the rules.
With heads held high as one, we strode around the ship of fools.

Our Love is not a thoughtless gift of passion for a night.
In years to come, the Love we give will still be burning bright.

And when in time our race is run, we'll toast our Love and
Join the Son.

A Passing Love by Cesar Lista

A PASSING LOVE

A harvest moon was on the land when first I saw her face.
A sparkling drop of pure delight.
A rose in a desert place.

I gather now my thoughts and dwell upon those memories
and never from that day has one replaced the least of these.

Those eyes of clearest wonder take me deep inside my soul.
That voice full sweet as honey makes my broken heart a whole.

And I will never leave behind this vision in my life.
Although I know my love shall never come to be my wife.

Light of Love Cesar Lista

THE LIGHT OF LOVE

In the fall, it came to be the meeting of my life.
And no one near could really see the heartache and the strife.
The friendship grew and fall passed on as winter filled the scene.
As leaves fell deaf upon the ground, each echoed in my being.

She saw me, felt me all around, but I must conceal my heart.

Winter's just a season and it floated through my life.
Spring appeared and Love, it neared to grow and cover strife.
No more could I conceal my heart, a warm and brilliant glow,
Melting the ice of winter, filling the streams of my soul.

Still, there was another man who wished her for his wife.

Summer faded into view when life is rich and full.
But I discovered far too late.
She played me for a fool.
Still, I entered life and breathed deeply of
Love as it was,
Though lost, the invisible guide for my heart.

For her, in the absence of another, I have shone and never darkened.

P.K. Rankin

Love and Parting VickieLSK

LOVE AND PARTING

A parting thought, I bid adieu
to one so pure and sweet.
A gift of Love both strong and true
I lay before your feet.

To you I pledge my very heart and
all I've come to be.

I take with me the vision of your
radiant, caring eyes.
The memory of your loving heart as
big as all the skies.

The vision that I carry now is one
that never dies.

To you this pledge I gladly make,
no sacrifice too great.
A promise now I offer for your love
I'll not forsake.

I only ask of you your hand in
pure love I may take.

P.K. Rankin

My Love for Thee by Cesar Lista

MY LOVE FOR THEE

Thy name is as a song upon the wind, constant and unending.
For thy beauty, no equal may be found in all the earth.
A beauty unto mine eyes, yet infinitely more so to my soul,
lifting my spirit past the gray skies and into a world of joy and peace.

Serenity in thy smile; a small glimpse of heaven in thy loving eyes.
Would that I might be forever found in thy tender heart, and that,
made perfect by the sacrifice of the son, may never fail.

I dream, and yet, I know myself awake.
Let it be so, that in waking the dream be not disturbed
and in dreaming I may wake not.
Perchance, having been surrounded by thy love this brief moment,
I might linger a moment longer and in lingering may I ne'er depart.

Grant me, I ask, that which lies within thy power to give;
thy love, thy heart and I, at last, shall be content above all men.

Though the work of man's hands may crumble
and man himself return to dust,
my love for thee shall not perish.

In Christ I love thee and in that love no fault may be found.
Through the son my life received and this I share with thee.

Unlock the Door by Judy Rogers

UNLOCK THE DOOR

A kiss is but a token of emotion felt within.
A look of adoration, merely somewhere to begin;
not a firm foundation, but a shadow pale and thin.

That twinkle in my eye, you see,
is not a pledge 'twixt you and me.
That gentle touch you feel, sweet soul,
is not the one to make me whole.

Love, my dear, is far more real
then looks and kisses, we might steal.
Love is more than we can touch
and far more than we feel.

Love could be defined as more
like friendship with an open door.
For where the doors are locked,
my friend, Love will fail to enter in.

The doors I open wide, unbarred.
no locks to hold you out.
All I yield to you, my friend,
my love without a doubt.

THE HUMAN CONDITION

I'm not certain, but I believe there is no issue or circumstance more contentious than the human condition. Whether we address it with spiritual pursuits, religion, ideologies, science, government, philosophy, or psychology the vast array of views is staggering. It seems true that no two people view humanity in exactly the same way. Speak to a dozen individuals and you are likely to get a very different view from each on how we should view, navigate, and improve it. I think it comes down to the answer we got from our creator from the beginning. We received paradise and free will. In answer to that, mankind chose free will. We are a stubborn and unrepentant lot. We are also fiercely independent. In the end, however, we each choose for ourselves.

The Standard by Cesar Lista

Thoughts & Musings

THE STANDARD

It is the scale by which we measure art.
Evolving with each generation and yet,
Timeless in all respects.

Always it lies in the eye of the beholder.
Some, however, presume to restrict
Or mold what is personal.
Beauty cannot be manipulated.

We paint it on, flaunt it like a prize
To be bragged on.
Never a thought for those whose beauty
Is dead before it is born.
Still, what of the beauty of life,
Shrouded and unseen by the physical eye?

Where we live it is cheap, not appreciated; expected.
We live in a corridor, travelling from one end to another
Never so much as pausing at the doors we pass,
Fearful of what we might find beyond.

Our ignorance does not negate its existence,
It is simply ignorance.

What of the girl in Somalia with no thought
For beauty, only hunger and living?
What of the boy in Bosnia fearing only for his life
And not another's perception of his looks.

Have we so little concern for what matters,
So caught up in our vanity that the true beauty,
The standard by which we are all measured,
Is no longer a standard but a casualty?

There is no standard, only Christ.
And through him all beauty is revealed.

The Heart of Man by Cesar Lista

THE HEART OF MAN

In the heart of every one of us a
darkness doth abide.
With love and care do some of us
the darkness seek to hide.

Yet covering a wound alone
won't make it go away.
So how then does a man propose
to hide his hate today.

When then shall mankind awake
to this travesty called life.
Must the whole world first be shaken
by the giant known as strife.

The homeless breed the hungry
and the rich deny the poor.
The masses fight for money
and death is at the door.

Our salvation lies in realization
our eyes must soon be opened.
For every man in every nation
must let his heart be softened.

As one consigned to harmony
man must seek to fell the giant,
Strife must live no more.

Woman by Judy Rogers

WOMAN

Fluid movements mark her presence,
Grace at her command.
Time and again you learn the truth,
Alone you cannot stand.

Your life becomes and endless struggle,
Each day a living hell.
Your fortress lies about in rubble,
She'll have your heart as well.

It does no good to make demands,
You can't resist her will.
Escape you may to foreign lands,
But she shall find you still.

A Demon, she is, of darkest black,
An Angel of purest white;
The strength and fortitude you lack,
You can't withstand her might.

So you must have her for your own
The final defeat already known.

Those Times by Cesar Lista

THOSE TIMES

There have been times when I cried out from the depths
of my very soul. There were times my heart was frozen
by that cruel unearthly cold.
Still, those times have always passed for I was never once
alone.
For even on the darkest night, to the depths of Hell and
back, my Lord
gave me the strength and courage I had always lacked.
The road I travel leads me to the valleys deep and wide,
to times of trial and trouble with no relief in sight.
This road winds also upward to the peaks amidst the sky
where the troubles of my life are far too heavy for to climb.

I have witnessed life and living, had my back against
the wall.
I have gone beyond the limits when this life has harshly
called. Yet all is now behind me since my Lord has
conquered all.
My Lord gave me new life to live, new roads on which
to tread.
I no longer fear the giving as the man I was is dead.

Pity by Cesar Lista

PITY

I personally don't believe in pity. It's a useless emotion if there ever was one, right up there with hate and avarice.

The latter two will eat you alive from the inside and destroy you in the end because they are consuming masters with no room for anything else.

Pity, however, is so much more devious when you open your soul to it. If you are tempted to pity someone, you would do better to find a way to comfort or aid them instead.

Pity is more a condescension in my eyes; something we wield to reinforce our own sense of goodness and that is all that it can do; it certainly doesn't help the person we pity.

Worse yet, is self-pity. If pity is useless, then self-pity is positively degenerative. I don't believe in it, and I don't accept it from others.

Thoughts & Musings

THE BATTLE

The stars upon the midnight sky and I at center stage;
The battle of my heart and mind within my soul
doth rage.

In turmoil born and thus conceived, in turmoil
do we die.
The struggle of the heart and mind shall ever light
the sky.

My heart denounces reason while my mind
pronounces thus.
Mine eyes I turn to heaven for the peace t
hat never was.

The mind says, "Here are answers, glorious
knowledge once foretold."
The heart cries, "Grasp it's beauty, not the
knowledge hard and cold.

Galaxies and Quasars, Suns that rise and stars
that fall.
In my mind, these wonders beckon that clear note of wisdom's call.

Timeless depths await thee. Come with me and
gaze in awe,
'pon the loving work of God's own hand,
not some scientific law.

A moment then to ponder on the path that
I should take;
shall I embrace the heart or mind,
the other to forsake.

The mind without the heart will die,
turned in upon itself.
The heart without the mind will lie
forgotten on the shelf.

Herein lies the wisdom of the ages come and gone.
Knowledge without beauty is a hollow, mournful song.

Therefore, advocate not one love, that of
science or of art.
Give thyself to each a portion of your mind and of your heart.

Thoughts & Musings

The Battle by Cesar Lista

The Game by Cesar Lista

Thoughts & Musings

THE GAME

Forever young, forever proud, forever more in love.
For today we live,
for tomorrow we plan our hopes
 the snow-white dove.

With destiny, a game we play, to fate
surrendered dreams.
The joy of life, the life of one; meaningless alone.

For now, content to ride the storm,
to sway beneath the wind.
From first to last, with purpose strong,
the game we seek to win.

Yet all at last is futile when the heart must standalone.
In a world of mere illusion with
no love to call your own.

P.K. Rankin

My Son by VickieLSK

MY SON

Come here my son.
Sit with me and let us talk for a while.
Something has been troubling my heart,
there are things I wish to know.
When you were born into this family
I was filled with joy beyond measure.
The mere thought that you would love me
as I loved you was a song for my spirit.

I gave you life, I gave you my life.
All that I am I have bestowed on you;
my name, my love, the joy I feel is yours to share.
How have I hurt you?

When have I wounded you
so that you would turn from me?
At times you could not understand me,
those times will come again.

Still, I have not intentionally hurt you.
I know at times it is hard but,
I ask only that you trust me;
have faith.
No matter the circumstances
you are my child and I love you
beyond comprehension.
Lean on me and take comfort in my love.

THE HEART

A Heart. Amazing in the eyes of man.
So fragile a mere word might break it.
Quick to damage and slow to heal, at times.
Yet, handled gently, unassailable by the
harsh storms of life.

Those to whom we entrust it, often
fall short of their obligation.
And when we give it away it becomes
Lost, on occasion.
In times of crisis, we shelter it; frequently
to no avail.
Still, at all times we revere it; lest we forget
our very selves.

Unlike many of the varied aspects of life, it
cannot be bought or sold.
Nevertheless, we seem all too willing
to bet it on the long shot.
A practice we are eager to repeat, but often
regretful of.

We trust our heart to a fault even when our
mind disagrees. It is not unheard of for
one to follow one's heart to places even the most
courageous of warriors avoid. Even mortal danger
pales when compared with the joys of the heart.

How is it possible, then, that so integral a part
of our life, so gentle in caring, so strong in love,
so inspired in leadership, and so deep in concern
can hurt so deeply and leave tracks of pain so indelible
as to remain visible, even when faded to obscurity?

Open up and understand. We are hurt deepest by those we
cherish most. At any cost we are willing to endure the
hurt, no matter the severity, for even the briefest
moment submersed in the healing waters of love.

Consider for yourself. Will you take the chance and
endure the pain at times to taste the victory or will
you conceal your heart for safety and accept the endless
pain of the LONELY HEART.

Thoughts & Musings

The Heart by Cesar Lista

The Last Knight by Cesar lista

THE LAST KNIGHT

As morning dawned upon the field, with armor gleaming bright.
The banners one by one unfurled; each visor was shut tight.
Polished blades from scabbards slid to cleave the morning air.
The battle cry did then arise, a song both loud and clear.

Their shields did flash, their lances poised, great swords were held up high.
Chargers hooves did echo then, resounding 'cross the sky.
Like ocean waves against the cliff they met upon the field; the clash of arms
And mail clad horse, the high-pitched ring of steel.

Armor rent, lances shattered, horses lost their riders.
Swords released from lifeless hands as souls did mount the skies.
The battle lasted days, it seemed, as the tide turned round about.
Each Knight strove to his dying breath then fell with a mighty shout.

Yet all at last was silence as the final foe did fall.
The carnage then was over, as one Knight had conquered all.
One lone figure standing 'midst the blood of friend and foe,
He knelt beside his standard there and whispered soft and low.

"Today I am the victor for my country and my King.
Still I ask you, Lord my God, forgive me for this thing.
The enemy defeated yet, no glory have I found.
No peace has come upon my heart though I am homeward bound.

I pray Lord grant me courage and the strength that you did show,
When they scourged you nailed you to a cross and laid your body low.
Keep me strong and brave my Lord, above all proud and true,
That I might join with Heaven's host and wield this sword for you.

The Last Knight raised his head and gazed into the morning sun.
Gave he then his final breath, the Lord's will had been done.

Feelings of Thought by Cesar Lista

FEELINGS OF THOUGHT

So many thoughts, tangled amidst these feelings with which I struggle.
So many feelings, hindering the process of thought.
Hopelessly entwined, yet separate;
Each leading a life independent of the other.

Always destined, however, to meet at some point,
or points, along life's highway.
Incapable of disengaging them,
yet powerless to reconcile these sides of myself
I have long since ceased to struggle.
The tumultuous relationship continues;
joined and divided throughout its course.
Never, at last, farther apart than ideals.
Perhaps ideals are the key.
Render these concepts invalid
and it might be that the problems
with the preconceptions shall disappear.

The Final Hour by Cesar Lista

THE FINAL HOUR

As lightning stretches from sky to earth
the visions on my mind's eye burst.
Of Heaven and Hell in a time to come
when the stage is set at last.

The gates are open, the crossroads clear.
The day brave soul we sought is here.
The proof requested now abounds
as evil meets its end.

The prophet of lies is revealed as such.
The man of peace has lost his touch.
And one more moment will be the plea
but the clock has ceased to run.

Where shall they hide, the dead inside,
those lost to a world of hate.
When time is full, and the clouds roll back;
then friend, it's far too late.

The time is now to turn the tide,
wait not for the final hour,
when fire and death and the gates of Hell
the faithless soul devours.

ABOUT THE AUTHOR
P.K. Rankin

Father, husband, worker, traveler, philosopher, lifelong learner, poet, and dreamer who believes in the adage that you can do anything you put your mind to. He is a lover of freedom and a respecter of life. An eternal optimist, stating that there is nothing in his world that could keep him down and nothing he would encounter that could destroy his soul. And adheres to the creed of never engaging in actions that you wouldn't be willing to sign your name to and never taking what you haven't earned.

Raised in a family rich in patience, love, and discipline more than money, they taught him to never be afraid of hard work. He internalized that advice, and ventured into professions such as a construction worker, laborer, truck driver, insurance processor, schoolteacher, merchant marine, and computer programmer. From his parents, he also learned to respect everyone and to fear God. To judge a man by his actions and integrity, but never by his skin or appearance. And to treat women with respect and hold them in the highest regard.

This book of poetry is his first published work; but stated that he began writing poetry, song lyrics, speeches and greeting cards as a teenager to vent his emotions. He writes for himself and hopes others find something enjoyable or useful in it.

Author PK Rankin lives in Florida with his wife and children. He travels to visit with family regularly in other parts of the country and enjoys music, writing, reading and an awful lot of hockey.

Reach out to him at: www.pkrankin.com

writer@pkrankin.com

X(twitter)@RankinPK

FAIRVIEW PRESS MEDIA Mgt.

Making your journey from writer to published author as easy as possible. From first-time authors to experienced veterans, we've helped prove that it doesn't take a traditional publishing deal to bring a dream to life.

The only thing we need from you is a manuscript. We can handle the rest. Have cover art? We can use your cover design, or we can design a cover for you. Whether you need the works or have prepared everything yourself and are ready to go to print, Fairview Press Media has everything you need for a successful publishing experience.

Contact us Today:

info@myfvp.com

www.https://fairviewpressmedia.com

Made in the USA
Columbia, SC
28 December 2023

933945aa-9fce-40f7-a777-dd0b22aaeac3R01